WHITE WORK

Techniques and
188 Designs

Selected and Edited by
CARTER HOUCK

Dover Publications, Inc.
New York

Published in Canada by General Publishing Company, Ltd., 30 Lesmill Road, Don Mills, Toronto, Ontario.
Published in the United Kingdom by Constable and Company, Ltd., 10 Orange Street, London WC2H 7EG.

White Work: Techniques and 188 Designs, first published in 1978, is a new collection of patterns from *The Chief Pattern Book of Embroidery Patterns for the Improvement of Artistic Embroidery on Linens and the Promotion of Good Handicrafts,* originally published in Nuremberg, Germany by the Johann Merkenthaler Factory (circa 1900). A new introduction has been written especially for this edition.

International Standard Book Number: 0-486-23695-1
Library of Congress Catalog Card Number: 78-56767

Manufactured in the United States of America
Dover Publications, Inc.
180 Varick Street
New York, N.Y. 10014

CONTENTS

INTRODUCTION

For most modern women the term White Work brings to mind visions of lacy, intricate pieces of embroidery obviously worked under a magnifying glass and too formidable to contemplate beyond the glass display cases of a museum. This vision is not necessarily true. White Work, which simply means white embroidery on white fabric, has long been a part of the embroidery tradition of many countries around the world. Since there must always be a smooth, even quality to the stitches that makes them blend perfectly with the background, White Work has always been the best way to show one's talent in needlework. Whether the embroidery is composed of a few simple stitches or looks like elegant lace, the techniques are basically the same. Fortunately, a little time and practice with the basic stitches can produce a very fine piece of White Work.

This book is intended as an introduction to the craft of White Work. It contains simplified techniques, stitch instructions and 188 embroidery patterns for White Work. I have chosen mostly those designs which can be worked effectively in raised embroidery using one, two or three types of stitches. I have purposely omitted many patterns that involve open work, pulled thread or cut work because I feel that these techniques are books in themselves. (See Fangel, Winckler and Madsen: *Danish Pulled Thread Embroidery,* Dover 0-486-23474-6.) The designs are grouped according to the stitches which I feel work best for them. As you become more sure of your technique, you can use other stitches, allowing your imagination to be your guide. The designs are all taken from an early twentieth-century German pattern catalog and were originally intended for White Work.

A BRIEF HISTORY OF WHITE WORK

Probably the oldest known piece that could be called White Work is a Danish braided hairnet taken from a 3,000-year-old grave. From that time to the present, White Work has appeared in many different forms in the cultures of many countries. The endless interchange of types of White Work fabrics and stitches and ways of working often makes it hard to follow the exact progress of any specific variety. For instance, "tambour work," one of the most popular types of White Work, can be traced from the East, probably China, to France and England in the mid-eighteenth century. From there it spread over much of Europe and, of course, to America. Today we see a form of it on fine, white muslin blouses and shirts imported from India and Pakistan. It lends itself to long, trailing vines and flowers and magical animals and mystical birds.

True tambour work was so called because it was worked on an odd-looking round frame resembling a drum. The frame had an oval base, rather like half of a huge egg, which rested on the lap, leaving both hands free to work. The basic stitch is a chain stitch, worked very rapidly with a tiny hook. The thread is carried underneath the stretched fabric with the left hand while the right operates the hook in a motion similar to rug hooking. (The chain stitch has one thing in common with many types of continuous stitching, worked either by hand or machine; it can be pulled out even faster than it is worked.) A fine copy of tambour work can be made with a needle by following the directions for chain stitch on page 9 and by using either a hand-held hoop or a standing frame. It is one of the simplest and most effective types of White Work and can be used for all or parts of many of the designs in this book.

Throughout history queens and ladies, little girls, servants and women of the church executed their White Work embroidery on a variety of things and for a variety of reasons. Little girls in many countries and of most social classes were considered uneducated if they could not do a beautiful sampler of stitches by the time they were ten years old. Servants were often hired because of their skill with the needle. A maid probably felt more fortunate to go blind embroidering her mistress' dressing gowns than to grow old scrubbing floors. Queens and ladies not only had idle hours to kill but many, like Mary Queen of Scots, probably looked upon their handwork as a principal means of expression. In the church there was an endless need for beautiful ecclesiastical garments and fine, white altar linens, which were produced either by nuns or great ladies. The story is told that Queen Isabella would ride out to battle in the morning at the head of one of Spain's armies and sit in her tent at night embroidering beautiful White Work robes for her favorite archbishop.

In the eighteenth century White Work in the form of pulled thread work of such delicacy was produced in Denmark that it often competed with the beautiful laces made in that country. The two techniques used similar designs, and it sometimes takes an expert to tell bobbin lace from pulled thread work, sometimes known as needle lace or embroidered lace.

As the Victorians began to decorate every blouse, cap and fichu of fine, white fabric with fine, white stitches, the competition was on. What started out as "sewed muslin," using a few easy stitches, was pushed out of popularity by "Venetian embroidery" or "French embroidery" or "Ayrshire work" of increasing complexity. In the middle of the nineteenth century one of the most long-lasting types of White Work, called "broderie anglaise," entered the competition. It is a relatively simple cut work, with no intricate needle lace worked in the openings. We now know it as "Madeira work," usually embroidered in pale blue thread on fine, white linen, using only satin and buttonhole stitches.

From mainland Europe, all kinds of needlework traveled the world over in the age of expansion and colonization. It may have been taken on purpose—as in the case of Madeira work—to fill an economic need or to create an industry. Incidentally the thread was changed from white to pale blue in the migration from England to Madeira because the blue stood up better in the more tropical climate which tended to yellow a pure white thread.

In many other cases the work changed over the years, finally taking on the native characteristics of the new lands. The Dutch took White Work to South Africa where some of the finest and most intricate is still worked. The people of the Philippines, with their mixed cultural heritage, produced beautiful White Work with a special appearance gained from the use of their own very suitable *piña*, a sheer even-weave pineapple cloth. No one would dare travel to the Philippines and not bring back the beautiful men's shirts or ladies' handbags of this cloth, delicately decorated with lacy white embroidery.

White Work was extremely popular in America through the Victorian era and on into the twentieth century. Young ladies were taught to embroider handkerchiefs at an age that we would now consider unthinkable. By the time the camera came along fewer intricate lace and open-work stitches appear in the blouses, collars and cuffs that we see in early photographs of American women, but many other types of White Work are in evidence. Feather stitch—single, double, ad infinitum—was one of the most popular White Work stitches, and many exquisite christening gowns were worked entirely in satin stitch, stem stitch and French knots.

Artistic trends have always influenced people who work with needle and thread as well as those who paint on canvas. Today as "white on white" has become a popular modern art technique, White Work is enjoying renewed popularity. We may no longer wish to trim petticoats or decorate a fichu, but we can enjoy White Work as a purely artistic endeavor. "Do your own thing," applies now to needlework as it does to all artistic pursuits.

MATERIALS FOR WHITE WORK

A few simple supplies are all that is needed to get started doing White Work. You will need some type of hoop or frame, fabric and thread. In addition you will need needles which correspond to the size thread you are using.

Look over the variety of hoops and frames available. If you decide on starting with handheld hoops, you will need about three sizes. They are usually more practical than the larger standing hoops and frames for work on small, beginning pieces. When you decide to make large table linens, curtains or shawls, you will be more comfortable with the standing frames.

The original fabrics of White Work bore some names no longer recognizable to the modern woman, accustomed to synthetic fibers and ever-changing weaving techniques. If you were to go into your neighborhood store and ask for "Indian mull," "French muslin," or, for that matter, "long cloth" or "batiste," you would be met with a blank look and an emphatic, "No!" Embroidery thread was originally cotton or linen, both of which have become increasingly hard to find in high quality in recent decades.

Fortunately, there are signs of a return to natural fibers. Many fine shops, and especially those that deal in needlework supplies, are now carrying even-weave fabrics, fine cottons from India, and very good quality six-strand embroidery floss.

There are other fabrics that have been used, depending upon availability, the fashion of the period and artistic license. Where fine wools are easily available White Work is made most effective with fine, white crewel yarn. There was a vogue for romantic "Spanish shawls" in this country in the early part of the twentieth century. Some of the loveliest of these were white silk with heavily padded satin stitch, worked in white thread.

If you live in or near a large city, your search for the right fabric may be somewhat easier than if your only source of supply is the general store or a shopping-center fabric chain. Learn to look at labels, ask questions and generally make a pest of yourself—you might get good results if you are persistent. Pure cotton or pure linen is usually easier to work on than a blend with synthetics. Needlework stores and mail-order houses often carry cotton Hardanger cloth, an even-weave with a double thread, formerly made only of linen. Smooth even-weave linens, which used to be referred to as "art linen," are imported from Ireland, Belgium or Holland, but you may have to search through a lot of fabric or specialty stores to find them. Bleached cotton muslin, long a favorite of quilters, can be bought wherever quilt supplies are sold and is usually 100% cotton. If you happen to find a source for batiste, long cloth, or organdy, consider yourself lucky and lay in a supply.

Many companies manufacture six-strand embroidery floss. Different brands have different qualities, and almost the only way to find out which you prefer is by the good old trial-and-error method. Try three or four different brands by using a double strand, preferably on a close-woven cotton. Work a line of chain stitch, some satin stitch, and a few French knots. It shouldn't take you long to find which brand is made of too-short fibers, and therefore shreds and becomes fuzzy, which twists and knots and which slides smoothly through your fabric. It won't take you long to decide which brand is for you.

There are some beautiful silk threads coming on the market from Japan, again hard to find, but worth the hunt for a white monogram on a white silk scarf. Those marvelous stitches on Victorian crazy quilts were worked in silk pearl twist or a highly mercerized cotton pearl, which gives much the same effect and comes in several weights.

If you become interested in moving away from tradtional fabrics and threads, you may find perfect backgrounds for your needle art in an art supply store among the heavy linens or other fabrics meant for painting. Upholstery and drapery fabric stores are also a fine source of fabrics with a lot of character. Wool, usually not a dead white, is a very interesting fabric, especially for wool yarns in several shades of white. You can embroi-

der on these fabrics with anything from the best Persian crewel yarn to slubby, nubby Scandinavian knitting yarn, heavy-weight pearl cotton, or cords and yarns that are made for macramé or weaving. The more weights, shades and types you have on hand to try out, the more original and interesting the finished effect. Texture is extremely important, especially in "white on white."

TRANSFERRING THE DESIGNS

In White Work the problems of transferring a design onto fabric are more obvious than in any other embroidery. Blue is the only acceptable color because other dark colors have a greater tendency to remain as ugly smudges, whereas blue will eventually blend into the white thread. The most desirable type of marking is one which washes out quickly after it has served its purpose.

Notions companies have tried to produce a blue marker that will wash out of white fabric. Two markers which I have tested seem to meet this criterion will. They are made by Dritz® and are available at most notions counters. There is a washable blue carbon (style number 636) and a refillable tailor's chalk pencil (style number 678) with refills (style number 679).

It is impossible for anyone to guarantee that even these fine products will wash out of every washable white fabric, or dry clean out of those that require dry cleaning. Testing is the best way to ascertain the combined qualities of marker and fabric. Make several legible but not too dark lines on the edge of your fabric and then rinse it in tepid water with a soap or detergent recommended for fine fabrics. When you are testing dry-clean-only fabrics, you will need the cooperation of your friendly neighborhood dry cleaner.

If your fabric is thin enough to see through, you can lay it over the design page, clip or pin it smoothly in place, and trace it with the chalk pencil. The chalk can be sharpened to a fine point with a single-edged razor blade whenever it becomes dull.

If the fabric is too heavy for you to see through, trace the design from the page onto tissue paper or transparent tracing paper (available in stationery or art supply stores). Use a cardboard cutting board or a piece of heavy corrugated box on which to pin the fabric flat. Pin the blue Dritz® Tracing Paper on the fabric and the tissue with the design in place on top of the blue paper. Use a very fine, very hard pencil and work lightly to impress the design on the fabric.

STITCHES
FOR
WHITE WORK

STITCHES FOR WHITE WORK

STEM or OUTLINE

This is the basic stitch used to define a line. It is worked from left to right but the needle is put into the fabric from right to left. Bring the needle

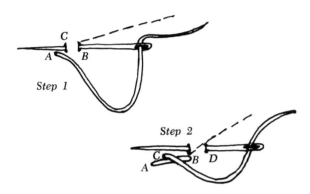

Step 1

Step 2

up through the fabric at A, put it in again at B (this is the length of the stitch as it appears on the surface of the fabric). Bring the needle out again almost half way back to A at C. Put it in again at D (the same stitch length from C as the A-B length) and bring it out almost back to B. The needle as it goes under the fabric can slant very slightly. The thread must always be kept to the same side of the needle, below for stem and above for outline.

CHAIN

A heavier definition of line can be produced with chain. It can also be used round and round, closely spaced, as a filler. Bring the needle up

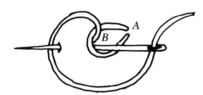

through the fabric at A. With the left thumb, hold the thread in a loop on the surface of the fabric, inserting the needle again at A and bringing it

out at B through the loop. Pull the thread gently and not too tightly to the left, hold another loop and insert the needle at B again. The loops should never be pulled into a straight line but should be softly rounded in appearance.

LAZY DAISY

This is a single chain stitch, often used as a small flower petal or leaf. The thread is brought

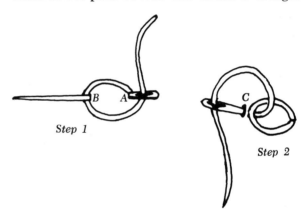

Step 1

Step 2

over the end of the loop and the needle inserted at C, about one thread beyond B, to hold the loop in place.

RUNNING

The first stitch that most people learn in sewing is the running stitch, an evenly spaced in-and-out line from right to left, good for joining seams. In

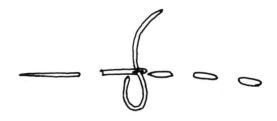

embroidery it is most used as a base for other stitches, to define and hold a line, or to pad an area to be covered with heavier stitching.

BACKSTITCH

This is another line-defining stitch, lighter and straighter in appearance than either stem and outline or chain. The line flows from right to left and the needle is run into and out of the fabric in that direction but is carried back from left to right between every stitch. Bring the needle up through the fabric at A (one finished-stitch length from the beginning of the line) and insert the

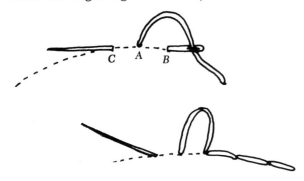

needle at B (on the beginning of the line). Bring it up again at C (one stitch-length to the left of A). The needle will always be inserted at the end of the preceding stitch.

STRAIGHT STITCH

The straight stitch is a hard one to define, though a simple one to work. It appears in so many guises that it is sometimes almost unrecognizable.

The running stitch is really a straight stitch, but the way in which it will be used most in White Work is in a fan arrangement, creating a circle like a delicate flower. Straight stitch and backstitch are used in infinite combinations to form the latticed effects of Blackwork.

SEEDING

The seed stitch is a delicate filling stitch, which must be worked in relatively heavy thread and

spaced evenly to be effective. It is a short straight stitch, always worked in groups at many angles, just as scattered seed would fall; hence the name.

SATIN

This is the trickiest of stitches for the beginner, partly because it looks deceptively simple. The aim is to cover a small to medium-sized area with smooth stitches, lying closely against each other, and forming an even edge. In leaves and other elongated shapes, it may be easier and more effective to work on a slant, rather than straight across the area.

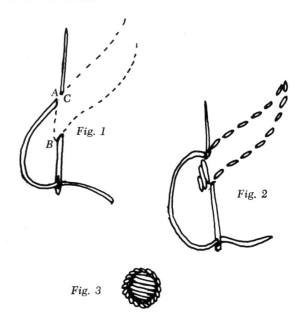

Fig. 1

Fig. 2

Fig. 3

Bring the needle out of the fabric at A, down at B, up again at C (as close as possible to A) while moving out along the outline of the design (Fig. 1). Continue following the design outline, holding the thread in parallel lines, as close together as possible.

It may help to use a running stitch or backstitch around the edge first to define the line (Fig. 2). Practice is absolutely necessary with each new fabric and thread combination. Work samples trying different thicknesses of thread, different angles, etc., until you are satisfied. When all else fails, and your finished piece has a ragged edge, try covering it with a very fine line of chain stitch or backstitch (Fig. 3). Never attempt satin stitch, even for a sample, without a hoop or frame.

PADDED SATIN

In larger areas, padding gives satin stitch a fuller, richer appearance. For heavy padding lay down one layer of satin stitch and then work

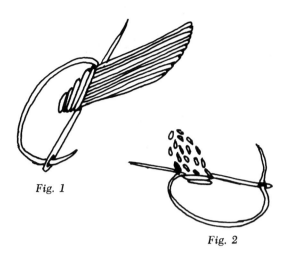

Fig. 1

Fig. 2

another one over it *(Fig. 1)*, either straight across or at a 45° angle. If you want a lighter padding, use a running stitch or backstitch around the edge and then back and forth across the area, as lightly or heavily as you wish *(Fig. 2)*.

LONG-AND-SHORT

If an area is too broad for satin stitch, long-and short should be used. It is a step beyond satin in difficulty and should not be attempted until satin is mastered. It is most suitable not only for large areas but for areas in which the color is to be shaded, and therefore more effective in colored embroidery than in White Work. You will find it helpful to outline the edge first as suggested for satin stitch. Work as for satin but with every other stitch about two-thirds of the length of the alternating ones. Work the next row in stitches of all

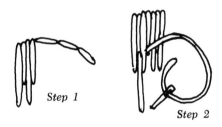

Step 1

Step 2

the same length. (They will still be uneven in apperance on the unfinished edge because they must touch the long and short stitches above them). If the fabric is loosely woven, the stitches may create a small hole where the ends meet. To avoid this and keep a smooth surface, work all the way into the ends of the stitches in the previous row. As you progress to fan shapes and other uneven shapes, you will find it necessary to add extra little stitches like wedges to accomodate a widening area, or to eliminate stitches to accomodate a narrowing area.

FRENCH KNOTS

Bring the needle up through the fabric at *A* and pull the thread up firmly. With the left hand wrap the thread around the needle from the eye end toward the point end, one, two, or three

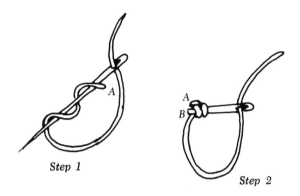

Step 1

Step 2

times. Insert the needle into the fabric at *B* (about one thread away from *A*). Let all the wraps of thread slide down the needle so that they are close to the fabric, and pull the needle to the wrong side, securing the knot of thread against the surface. For practice, start with one wrap and work up to the larger numbers.

OVERCAST
(for eyelet)

The overcast stitch is used rather loosely in hand sewing but in embroidery it must be worked very closely and evenly. The stitch is made by bringing the needle up through the fabric a few threads back from the edge, over the edge, up

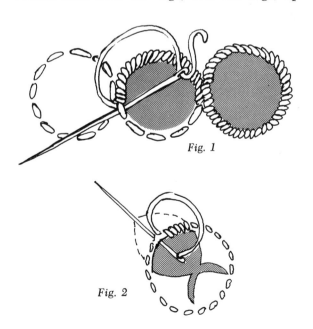

Fig. 1

Fig. 2

again close to the first stitch and the same depth from the edge, and over again, until the entire fabric is covered.

For added support and slight padding make a row of close running stitches around the marked opening. On many fabrics the opening can then be cut away with fine scissors and the overcasting worked immediately without fear of raveling (*Fig. 1*). If the fabric is so sheer as to need further support, cut across the opening in perpendicular lines and fold the triangles of fabric back (*Fig. 2*), trimming them away after working the overcast through the doubled edge.

BUTTONHOLE
(also used for eyelet and scallops)

This stitch can be worked openly for a lacy effect or very closely, to be used like the over-cast in broderie anglaise. The stitches form three sides of a square when worked openly; out of the fabric at A, in again at B (diagonally opposite corner of square) and out again at C. The thread must be looped and held under the needle as it comes out at C, then pulled firmly but gently into place as the needle goes in again at D and out at E.

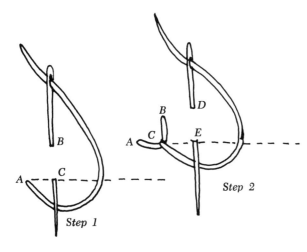

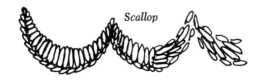

Scallop

The advantage of buttonhole stitch in cut work is that it can be worked along the line of the design, very closely, and the fabric trimmed away afterwards. On scallops the stitches graduate in width from the corners to the center of the scallop and back again. They can be padded with running stitches to create a heavier edging.

NOTE: *This last group of stitches is used for fillers and as borders or frames. The stitches give you a chance to vary your work and dress it up in true Victorian style.*

FEATHER

Think of the basic feather stitch as two rows of interlocking triangles. Bring the needle up through A, straight across to the right and into the fabric at B, and out again at C (the third point of the triangle with A and B). Loop the thread and hold it under the needle, as in the buttonhole stitch. Swing to the left, into the fabric at D and out at E (forming another triangle with C). Swing back to the right (forming another triangle, E-F-G).

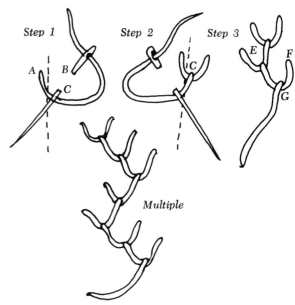

Multiple

Multiple rows of feather stitch are formed by going two or three stitches to the right and then the same number to the left. The angle of the triangles can be varied for narrower or wider effects by starting with A and B closer togther or farther apart.

HERRINGBONE

This is a simple border stitch or can also be used in multiple rows as a filling. The needle goes

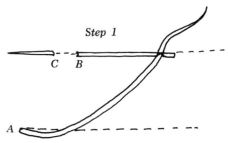

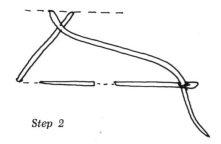

Step 2

in and out of the fabric from right to left but the line of stitching progresses from left to right. It is worked between two parallel lines. Bring the needle up through the fabric at *A* on the left end of one line, carry it diagonally across to the right and put it in at *B* on the other line, taking a small stitch under the line and bringing the needle back out at *C*. Cross diagonally to the right to the other line and take another stitch from *D* to *E*. Continue back and forth between the lines, being sure to keep the angles the same and the stitch lengths even.

CHEVRON

This is another border or filling stitch, worked diagonally between two lines. Bring the needle up through the fabric at *A* (the left end of one

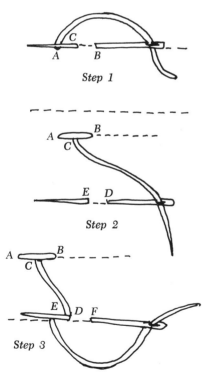

Step 1

Step 2

Step 3

line). Insert the needle into the fabric at *B*, on the same line, and take a small backstitch to *C* (one-half of the distance from *A* to *B*) holding the thread away from the parallel line. Insert the

needle diagonally to the right on the other line at *D* and take a small stitch to the left, bringing the needle up at *E*, to the right and down into the fabric at *F*, making a stitch along the line the same length as the *A-B* stitch. Continue along the line, alternating straight and diagonal stitches.

STAR

You will find this a versatile stitch for small round spots, tiny flowers, or as a filling. Use a circle as a base. Work a vertical and a horizontal

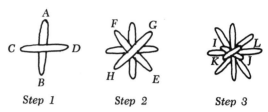

Step 1 *Step 2* *Step 3*

stitch, *A-B* and *C-D*, across the circle, then two diagonal stitches, *E-F* and *G-H*. Tie them together with a small tight cross at the center, working between the horizontal and the diagonal stitches, *I-J* and *K-L*.

SHADOW

This is a stitch used almost exclusively on White Work, especially on very sheer fabrics, such as organdy. Because it is worked on the wrong side of the fabric, the effect depends on the stitches showing through strongly, so use a fine washable yarn or at least four strands of six-strand em-

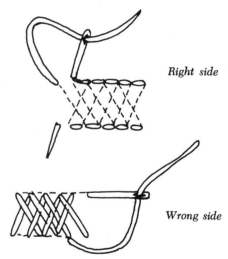

Right side

Wrong side

broidery floss. On the wrong side of the fabric work a very close herringbone stitch. The resulting horizontal backstitches along the parallel lines will be on the right side of the fabric and the ends should exactly meet, making two solid lines enclosing the shadow effect.

13

COUCHING

This is not a stitch which will be used much in traditional nineteenth-century White Work but will be a necessity if you try a more modern approach of white on white needle painting. It is generally used for holding down a line of heavier

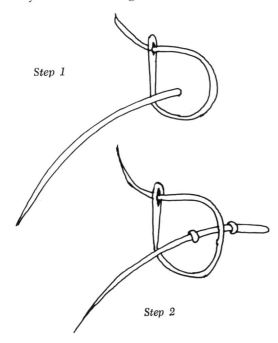

Step 1

Step 2

thread with stitches of a lighter one. Bring the heavy thread up through the fabric at the beginning of the line and hold it along the line with the left hand. With a finer thread take small stitches across the heavy thread at distances of from ¼″ to ½″. Conceal the end of the heavy thread by pulling it back through the fabric to the wrong side.

LATTICE FILLING

This makes an excellent light filling in threads of any weight. It is worked in a similar manner to couching. The base thread is brought out through the fabric, laid all the way across the area to be filled, brought through to the wrong side, back out about ¼″ away and across in a parallel line, A-B, C-D, until the area is covered. Lay rows of

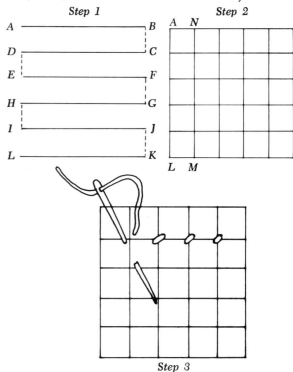

Step 3

threads perpendicular to the first ones, forming a checkerboard effect. Use small couching stitches across each corner intersection at a diagonal angle to hold the long threads in place.

DESIGNS FOR WHITE WORK

Stem or Outline
Satin
French Knots
Lattice

Stem or Outline
Satin
French Knots

Chain
Padded Satin
Buttonhole Scallop
Backstitch

19

Straight
Feather
French Knots

Lattice and Couching
Straight
French Knots
Backstitch

Lazy Daisy
Seeding
Satin
Stem or Outline

Stem or Outline
Chain
Satin

23

Stem or Outline
Satin
Padded Satin
French Knots
Seeding

24

Lazy Daisy
Overcast Eyelet
Stem or Outline
Satin

Lazy Daisy
Long-and-Short
Satin
Chain

Long-and-Short
Satin
Chain
Padded Satin

Lazy Daisy
Chain
Seeding

28

Stem or Outline
Satin
Padded Satin
Seeding
Lattice

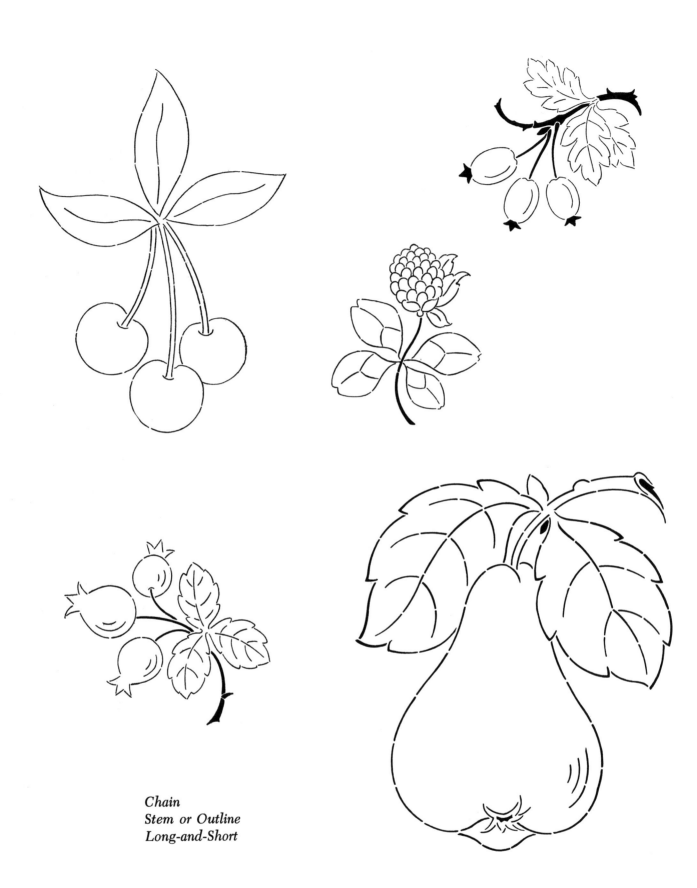

Chain
Stem or Outline
Long-and-Short

Backstitch
Chain
Satin
Padded Satin

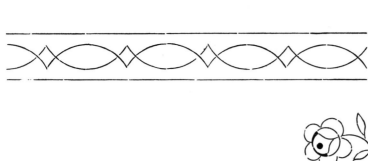

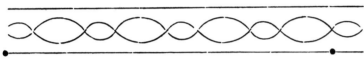

Chain
Lazy Daisy
French Knots

Chain
Stem or Outline

Buttonhole
Straight
Chain
French Knots

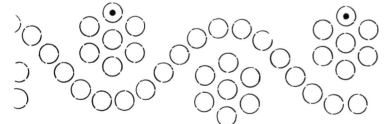

Overcast Eyelet
Stem or Outline
Lazy Daisy
Satin
French Knots

35

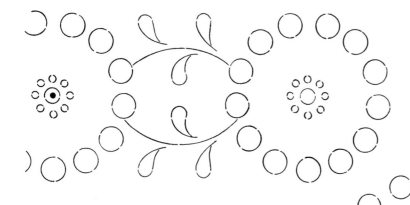

Overcast Eyelet
Satin
Stem or Outline

Chain
Satin
Long-and-Short
Overcast Eyelet
Chain
Satin

Satin
Stem or Outline
Lattice
French Knots

38

Satin
Stem or Outline
Lattice

Overcast Eyelet
Satin
Stem or Outline
French Knots

40

Buttonhole Scallop
Satin
Backstitch

Straight
Backstitch
Satin

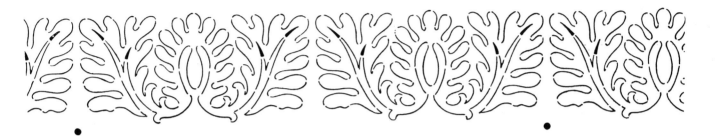

Chain

43

Stem or Outline
Satin
French Knots

Chain
Straight
French Knots

Stem or Outline
Satin
French Knots

46

Stem or Outline
Chain

47

Chain
Lazy Daisy
French Knots

48

Chain
Satin
Straight

49

Stem or Outline
Chain

50

Chain
Overcast Eyelet
Satin
Chain
Satin

Chain
Overcast Eyelet
Satin
Backstitch
Long-and-Short

Stem or Outline
Overcast Eyelet
Satin

Buttonhole Scallop

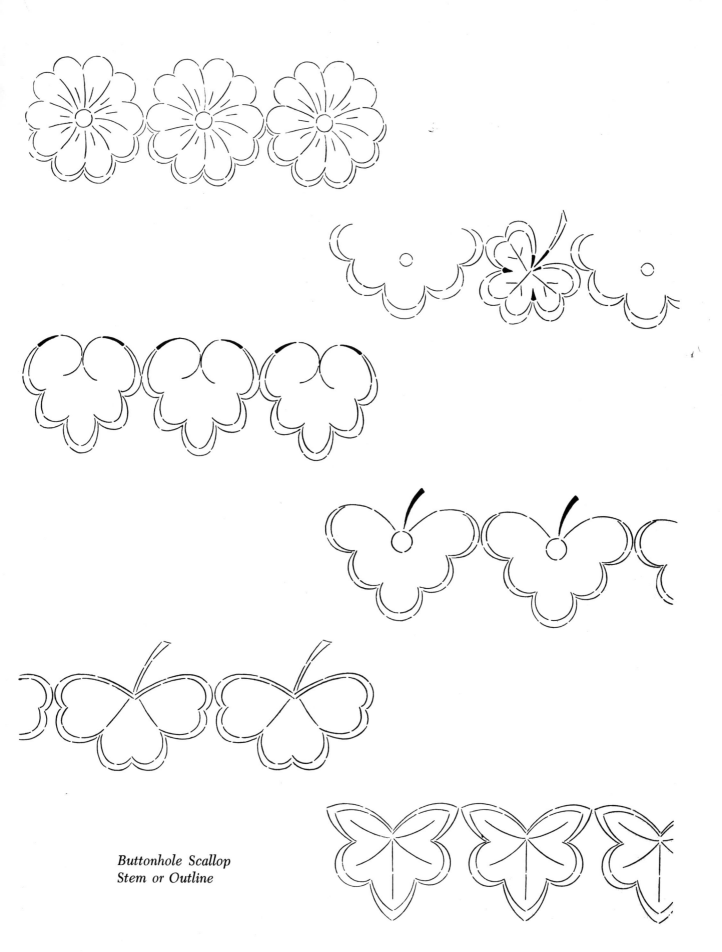

*Buttonhole Scallop
Stem or Outline*

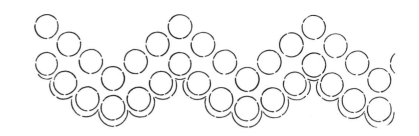

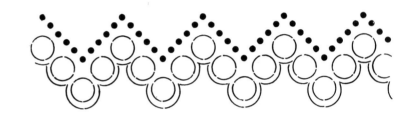

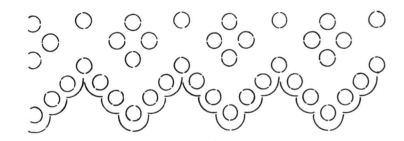

Stem or Outline
Buttonhole Scallop
Overcast Eyelet
Satin

Stem or Outline
Buttonhole Scallop
Overcast Eyelet
Satin

A . B . C . D . E . F .

G . H . I . J . K . L . M . N . Q .

. P . R . S . T . U . V . W . X . Y . Z .

A . B . C . D .

E . F . G . H . J .

K . L . M . N . O .

P . R . S . T . U . V .

W . X . Y . Z .

58